MW01093212

BY THE SAME AUTHOR

Moonshots (poetry), Beirut 1966.

Five Senses for One Death (poetry), The Smith, New York 1971.

"Jebu" suivi de "L'Express Beyrouth - Enfer" (poetry),
    P. J. Oswald, Ed., Paris 1973.

Sitt Marie-Rose (novel), Des Femmes, Paris 1978.

Sitt Marie-Rose (novel), The Post-Apollo Press, Sausalito, Ca.
    1982. Editions in Arabic, Dutch, Italian, German and
    Urdu.

L'Apocalypse Arabe (poetry), Papyrus, Paris 1980.

Pablo Neruda Is a Banana Tree (poetry), De Almeida, Lisbon 1982.

From A to Z (poetry), The Post-Apollo Press, Sausalito, Ca. 1982.

The Indian Never Had a Horse & Other Poems (poetry),
    The Post-Apollo Press, Sausalito, Ca. 1985.

Journey to Mount Tamalpais (essay), The Post-Apollo Press,
    Sausalito, Ca. 1986.

The Arab Apocalypse (poetry), The Post-Apollo Press, Sausalito,
    Ca. 1989.

The Spring Flowers Own & The Manifestations of the Voyage
    (poetry), The Post-Apollo Press, Sausalito, Ca. 1990.

Paris, When It's Naked (fiction), The Post-Apollo Press,
    Sausalito, Ca. 1993.

Of Cities & Women (Letters to Fawwaz), The Post-Apollo Press,
    Sausalito, Ca. 1993.

THERE

*In the Light and the Darkness of
the Self and of the Other*

Library of Congress Cataloging-in-Publication Data

Adnan, Etel.
    There : in the light and the darkness of the self and of the other
  / Etel Adnan.
        p.   cm.
    ISBN 0-942996-28-3
    I.   Title.
PS3551.D65T44   1997
818' .5407--DC21   96-52155
                                                    CIP

Copyright © Etel Adnan 1997
All rights reserved

The Post-Apollo Press
35 Marie Street
Sausalito, California 94965

Cover photo by Etel Adnan
Book design by Simone Fattal

Printed in the United States of America on acid-free paper.

THERE

*In the Light and the Darkness of
the Self and of the Other*

ETEL ADNAN

THE POST-APOLLO PRESS
Sausalito, California

ACKNOWLEDGEMENTS

Sections from *There* have appeared in *Lusitania* (special issue on Sarajevo), and in *Electronic Poetry Review* at http://www.poetry.org.

To the memory of Khalil Hawi

THERE

Where are we? where? There is a *where,* because we are, stubbornly, and have been, and who are we, if not you and me?

Where are we? Out of History, of his or her story, and back into it, out in Space and back to Earth, out of the womb, and then into dust, who are we?

Where is where, where the terror, the love, the pain? Where the hatred? Where your life, and mine?

There is a where, connected to telephone lines, a place for waiting, another for sleeping, a kiss and a flower, and where are we when you are, and where are you when I wait for you to be, be the people I see.

Who are we, a race, a tribe, a herd, a passing phenomenon, or a traveller still travelling in order to find out who we are, and who we shall be?

Are we travelling on a rope, is cancer eating our neighbors, where the sun when night descends, and where paradise on the ocean's asphalt roads?

Who are we, a woman or a man, and is that seasonal, is it eternal, and is it true that there are men and women and it must be true, because you are and I am.

Is there hatred in your heart, and does it mean that I am not here, and where are you when it's getting late?

To go, be going, straight ahead, the world being round, to be coming back, to where, to what, to be a bouncing ball, where, on what, to be defeated by gravity.

Who are you when you're not me, and who am I? Should we be people or fish, sharks, intelligent enough to wipe ourselves off the face of the earth?

And what is earth? some mud, some glue, a meteor, can it belong to itself?

Should you love me because I'm free, and should I follow your destiny instead of mine, out of History, away from Time and its satellites whose names are fear and death? Should I be?

Where are we? In the middle, at the beginning, the end? Who is we, is it you plus me, or something else expandable, explosive, the salt and pepper of our thoughts, the something that may outlast our divinities?

Am I always going by boat, and wherefrom? Am I crying, and why? Are the roads blocked by angels or by soldiers?

I'm asking you to run ahead of yourself and tell me why my bones are cold, or am I wanting you to leave my trees alone and search for water where the rivers overflow?

Going, into a train and stopping nowhere, because *it is* nowhere, with people pouring in, like ripped bags of wheat, birds helplessly flying overhead.

Who are we, us the children of History, whose, which period, which side of History, the wars or the poems, the queens or the strangers, on which side of whose History are we going to be? Are we going to be?

Where are we? In a desert, on a glacier, within a mother's womb or in a woman's eyes, in a man's yearning, or are we into each other, each other's future, as we have been in the past? Are we dead or alive?

I have never been here, where a pleasure boat rocks in the heat, and you have never been in my aunt's garden, where have you been then? We went out to look for you and you were sleeping by a fountain. Where was the moonlight? Where the anguish?

I threw my memories out the window and they came back,

alien, beggars and witches, leaving me standing like a sword. Is that why the sun is so bleak when it looks at us, and why is there so much love under the heat and the truth?

THERE

Oh yes! Columbus landed somewhere, where, bringing stench, disease and mortal wounds, logs to crucify Indians on, and when was it and why? So you're my twin enemy-brother, my twin shadow, and did we go to the Americas, who sent us there?

Go deep into the world's throat, there's no way out of this universe, but then is there a universe, and why, and where-from, and is its existence necessary for anything to *be,* and if there's not a somewhere what then, with no faith, no hope, there's maybe love, somewhere?

Are we calling the wind on the imagination's vast expanse, are you keeping my door closed or are you coming at night with the key, the food, the smile, the hatred and the love? Are you there in the dark?

Is a mountain meant not to move and is the sky to be wide open when we're sure to be, to be what, are we still alive when we're dead and are we here to stay? Do you know that I am here, like a river, a knife, or anything that you can buy and take home?

Where are we to go when the lights will go out and we'll look similar? We demand a reprieve from the drought but we're so afraid of water that the rain stops when it comes and we return to the sun.

The movement of the body, the heat, the fire, were fine, and where have the afternoons gone, why so many wars, why did Guevara unearth Columbus' bones?

And you speak to me of peace, over coffee, like in the old days, I mean between military campaigns, and nobody knows how the music was written, by whom, on whose table, and was it with ink or blood?

And you see we may go the way dinosaurs did, but we're here, aren't we, and God has preceded us into divine disappearance, aren't we reduced, suffering from too much visibility, multiplying in order not to be here, one day, a day like the first days, the stones being, being there, on the soil, the stones are not the end, the end of what, of whom, of you and me, and maybe only you and then only me, when it wouldn't matter anymore, the stones are the beginning.

THERE

In the earth's bowels we gather and project deadly operations, right here, regardless of the sea's decisions, and you appear amongst us - Maïakovsky in Vermeer's kitchen - bewildered: could anybody plan your death, could they kill your old neighbor, (would they prevent him from watching the news, that fatal night, would his soul look at his body lying in a pool of his own blood?), yes they will, and you would do the same, the killing comes first, the reasons, after.

We crossed jungles, do you remember, the dream was growing faster than the coconut trees, we were liberating the world from its failures. We buried Bolivian peasants next to the Che, reenacting Christ's story as far back as at the Amazon's sources. We went there. That voyage is stored in real memory.

He who counts the hours loses timelessness and we count our dead. It's always too late, too late for what, for the conversation we want to carry one late afternoon at Caffè Bugatti's, somewhere on the West Coast, away from the front line, but war is around us, visible at different degrees of sharpness. We always die on some well defined spot. The body goes.

Floods, as persistent as the sun could be. It is in the early mornings of the Bay that a peace I would share with you invades my awareness. The light steams out from the ground and carries the soul into a sensation of beginnings. Things seem possible, which have something to do with the thrust of living.

You may claim the privilege to such an experience. How to assess your mind's clarity, its innocence? It's clear there, over there, as I see it from my window, my brain getting sharper than a radio satellite. I don't need to travel if I wanted to visit the disappeared streets of my hometown, and you are doing the same, I'm sure, even if your birthplace stands gloriously under its flag, but you lost forever the particular light which accompanied you to school between ages four and six.

A street is territory borrowed from the past into which we engulf ourselves in search of transfiguration. In fact, we're engaged in the destruction of things we love because impatience is part of passion.

Dead, deadly, is death. Time is counted. Let us not measure love's weightlessness. Is there light ahead, any sky which lifts itself in its youthful fierceness?

THERE

And there sat our shadows facing each other, and were you behind the veil, the wall? Your eyes were absorbing the blueness of sorrow while I was looking at the Nile, the river starting at the horizon, coming down large terraces, frenzied, frightening, and a flower reached me, ate at my substance, became a butterfly goddess, and we went on, into a trance.

Can't we understand each other and stop the killing, without the dance, the run and the walk?

This morning? It's too early for the beach, too soon for starting a fight, so we linger on some light beam and go through windows, unnoticed, while the Police is waiting with sticks, gloves, gases, orders to shoot or not to shoot beyond one's brain, but can the Police stay calm anymore than a flower from the Nile can stop rising from the water and become a parachute, a World War II celestial machine which has already left for outer space? We're weak, sitting, facing each other, antlers locked in battle.

And I sat on the floor, O Shahrazade, with no king to do the listening, no beggar, and are you there, behind the curtains, beyond our mountains?!

Who is my enemy, and should I have one, is he my former friend, was he young when he came to slaughter, did he, mistakenly, shoot down his daughter?

The sun is above me, the original one that angels speak about, a ball of fire, look! There's dust over there, storms, there's love, which love, what for, there's SOMETHING over there which keeps growing ...

It's cold, over there, under primitive tents made of skins as soft as my heart's. You're so beautiful, young fellow, my eyes can't see you, so pale that your presence lights my house.

Look at us, although we don't know to whom we're speaking, you don't have to know me, when the wind blows it brings home your ephemeral beauty, before it's too late, and before we go on similar and different roads to where my mind will be racing faster than my thoughts.

Anyway, who are you? Born under a female sign, a warrior, woman or man, and does it matter when desire rises before we know it, telling things unknown?

You stand in front of me like death, or the last Word, made of time, speed ... You deported live flesh, made curses come to life and melt within our bones. Who can I call a friend?

Always, on the pleated horizon, there's fear, and some

instability runs like a god of earlier days, or the first thought-wave, and I'm in a hurry, aren't you too, you whom I can't call woman or man?

Are you transparent water like my eyes used to be, do I have the last word on this? Are you the Beast of the Apocalypse, needing a corn field for your wedding, your wedding? ...

They're shooting on the frontline, shaking the kids out of their sleep, as it happened already, over there, when nobody watches.

You live in the soul's darkness, somewhere in Southern Spain, where we were married, and divorced, where you got sick-leave, the Church looking down over our shoulders, when it was not crucifying us or burning our books.

Why do you bother with yesteryears now that we're going to the moon with rockets, beyond Mercury although not beyond our miseries, why grief, salt water, hunger?

The system is cracking, it's an implosion, the debris are human limbs, who cares?

You're facing me, aren't you, or you might not be there and I may have to go to the movies, where half of us go, the other half going to hell. But beware. Roles are interchangeable, and you keep sending me messages care of pelicans.

In this afternoon, this ominous moment, what answers do you have, what clash of wills are we fostering when we answer a bullet with a bullet, a thousand corpses with as many corpses? Who should feed the wolves?

There

In the here and now. We know the images and the words but where's the key and the link? An empire is crumbling, which one? A collapse is not a revolution, Russia is not redeemed, which Russia and for how long? Love and justice are the Messiah, isn't it?

60,000 children are missing in the United States alone, who's missing them, the government, the people, you and me, united in that private war waged within our boundaries, which boundaries, you may ask, those of the heart, this particular object with the red color of blood.

Living beyond the fog you're putting your calendar into order but pain doesn't need a treaty, political prisoners do not hear about diplomacy, they're behind bars because of the thought and the dare. Listen, over there in orange blossoms and bananas, in my neighbor's myrtle tree birds were singing freedom to the little girl I was, over there, and where are the bridges?

You know it and I do, that you lived where I did and we left on the same day in stormy weather. Where were you when war broke up, the one and the many, turning populations into long lines of sheep?

Should I explain what humiliation is about, have I not escorted you to the dead's domain, haven't we had conversations with ghosts, some we knew and some we didn't ...

Mud is of the essence, dear to creation, indigenous to a land of rivers, rivers of sperm and salt, and it makes houses too, over there, and it's covered with napalm and the American flag.

You speak of poetry, as they do in Arabia - sometimes to undercover agents. If words are not in the streets they're obsolete, you said it to me and I listened, while innocence was available.

I'm telling you, anger dies while fires survive, and before my family tree produces the olives you'll eat, there, in the heat the anger and the dust, stones will turn into leaves.

There

It rained blood. Holy cities caved in. Nobody watched the fires. Our imagination survived the onslaught; why it inflicted upon itself such terror we can't comprehend.

The terror is here, never relenting, the wind blowing, the sun orbiting. Where would it be if not amongst us?

Where is my love for you, hiding, watching over your sleep, combing your body with questions, getting ready for a wedding? Is it perchance sending announcements for a disaster? Is the human species persisting in its becoming?

THERE

And here, they can transplant my eye on your head or sew your hand on my arm, while we're light years away from each other because, somewhere, evil is wished on you, and you wished us to die, you the solitary being who struggles like a whale and me, i.e., Saturn and Mercury at war over the ocean.

In grey luminescence, on colored brain tracts, the hour is unsure, quivering there, over there, this time inside, or is it outside the core of one's being, as we always are *the other?*

Days are in military gear, Prometheus stole the fire, for whom, for what, for war? Whose wars are we fighting? I'm gasping for air, not gas, would these malignant clouds pass away, and the horizon burst open!

It's dark, it's after dark, we're linked by some ancient memory which is close to the experience of birth. Whose paradise shall paradise be?

In the heart's subways appetite could turn into poison, livid anger can mean blindness for the children, there, on death's playground, you could find my hand before it burns and disappears, while time is standing still.

THERE

The time is new and the page is white, light proceeds towards greater acuity, the day leads to the morning paper.

Go and sit there, your mother told you when she was young and you admired her hair and wished to be her little comb, I sat in a different garden, and we ate flowers, yellow lips giving us away.

Do you still have that taste in your mouth, should my heart slow down, wait, but why, now that we're dispersed, torn away from the old toys, they were too few, they carried illumination.

Would Nature put up with our agitation? Love is subversion, you told me, adding that it tortures the body out of its limits, and how sure were you of my love, do we need such turmoil for the business of daily life; these rivers will rise up to the sidewalks, light will obliterate the sky, then become thinner than fog, a most invisible desperation to be forgotten by all, and ourselves too …

You are. I would stop by, and the desert which I carry within will clear its storm. Last night the sky was impatiently beautiful, it took us beyond the things I'm telling you.

Where did we go? distance is a mystery. Why can't we go through, can we? Nothing is going to bring us together, so let us sit: a conversation is the beginning of civilization. We wanted an apotheosis, enough of that. Let's have coffee.

THERE

There, in this room, where there's pain, yes there is, I'm living pain and so are you, even if I didn't love you.

In front of the sea which is covered with blue meadows a line is trembling with fire, all over you, and you're facing me with guns, as you did with slings and stones, and why this grey metal over my head, and you turning toward darkness?

There are a few trees, the trees are few and fewer, fuel is filling your lungs, madness, your limbs. I'm not at one with the world anymore and let your heart not break, love will defeat the sound barrier in your veins and over the land's peaceful fields.

But things are always impossible, what of the possible and why the absence? Is the sea forgetting its epic tales?

Listen, listen if you care (or if you don't), do not mistake wine for food, do experience fear outside your mother's womb, remember with your guts, speak from *my* own heart, extricate yourself, if you can, from my rage.

There, along the white marble climbing toward heaven and

through a sky darkened with airplanes, listen, there's noise, the gates to nothingness are open while you struggle, and stutter, and I speak with no voice ...

In the thereness of time, a race to the sea, look, she's at my feet and you're standing under a deluge of hail, and nothing is growing, the wheat and the corn have ripened and are gone, and you're moving slowly, because between you and me there's space's infinity.

There, solar probes keep landing on my heart and create pure whiteness on my skin, galaxies churn in my stomach as well as in your belly, and there's no dance, the music is obliterated because a tree is fighting for its life in a nearby hospital.

Always beneath a smile lie the serpents of treason, and look how blue the morning is, my desire's last ocean! You barricaded yourself with memories of death while I listened to the doomed. And why all this, where have they all gone, boats, people, where? Always to a place we have already left. Cool springs meander through the cliffs of someone's country, never yours or mine.

Mountains are surrounding me, streams invade my plants, why don't they drown your hopes of conquest, overrun my father's grave?!

They're eating dry bread, over there, under Ra's auspices, and over here they're starving amidst opulence, and when you stand there, staring at them, they refuse to see that you're burning in a fire fed by stones. A dry riverbed, evil, not a bush, not a thorn ... here, and there, do meet in this river, this valley of the dead.

THERE

There, where you are (am I sure you're where I suppose you to be?), there's life, growth, it seems, shadows …

Around me there's life too, plenty, mosquitoes circling my chair, cockroaches in the basement, my curtains are of the best silk despite the poverty which radiates through the night and against which you invented rifles, you know what is well known, that we gather the poor behind the garbage then throw them with dustbins beyond the town's borders.

None of our gods are poor so how can we pray to them, where the promise, the suspended gardens? Why is the moon so shy now that we have measured her so carefully?

Listen. Again. The magic of words is working. There, on the other side, which side, we shall soon discover, a reef is probably rising, a boat entering the harbor, the captain has landed, I'll have a chance to trust him in spite of the cannon's roar, and some food has been served, and let's eat, while we're still hungry.

Terror, you're involved with terror, children know your

name, you're turning on the heat, where would your head lie when the noise should become unbearable, will it chase us out, out of this togetherness, away from the day's middle?

It was all meant to be: this pain, you mean, the mercury in the fish, poison coming to shore in our bones. My blood has cooled, it was beautiful here before you landed, you took notice, disturbed the mountains, the god's resting place; we had trees, which trees I'll tell you later, but they were all over the field of my vision, and you blurred that vision, why for …

THERE

Rivers mix anguish into their waters, the sea is iridescent, streaked with different hues, the ones I saw when I drove by, eyes half closed, oh the sun at an angle and the pink city hurrying to the horizon!

Desire rises and is still muffled, there, where your past piles dust on memories; where are the waves going insistently, yearning for the universe, the way you do, but are you moving toward anything?

My mind skids over things, this chair, this room, side streets, unfriendly encounters ... I wonder if your voice - your will? - could ascend to the sky, is the latter empty, are angels products of the earth ...

Now it's past noon, with salt in the sea, is your arm reaching me, are you there, invisibly swimming, or am I lost in a mist careful and friendly.

Oh how old is the space we live in, green, for just a few days, fading; tall reeds enliven the summer, and waves are jumping, where are the kids we didn't have, in spite of the beach, why such smoothness ...

Now you're coming, tell me, talk, is something falling, are we at war, is the land's thirst calling for blood, are clouds moving in pairs today? The mountain is spread and close to my nature, in its dryness, its age, its imperviousness to evil's armies. Are we both abandoned?

How would I make it clear that the sea is moving while I feel stillness and that the temperature rises in the streets with the level of desperation ...

There

When water and the sky meet space starts rolling back, coming
to terms with its origin, waiting to be reduced to duration,
and later, following in that direction, to flesh, blood, skin and
nails ... where in my body is there any room for all this?

The sparrow says "perhaps," then it says "I'm listening in," the
foghorn covers the ocean's voice. I'm bringing tons of paper
in my luggage and is America for real, I dream of it when I lose
hold. Is there anybody walking its broad plains, for a change?

And when is when, when the question, where the beat? ...
The ocean is entering through my window.

This cry doesn't break like glass, doesn't need an alphabet.
Your heart trembles along the walls of the city which gave
birth, oh yes, suddenly, under lightning, to light.

Transient is the bridge that will carry us to where the sun
doesn't set. In the air's pink granite mountains unfold. We
went up steep distances and energy was needed. We did not
fear the night although obscurity was dense and didn't assume
that the clouds would be benevolent. The impossible dream
visited our sleep. We did not awake to check on the dawn.

THERE

Such impotence in so much beauty, there ... Why are there so many prostitutes among the men; street corners, garbage, police and flies feeding on corpses, heat, narrowness?

Don't bargain for my possessions. They may not disappear. Here, around the house, defined perimeters keep the sea's roar away from my head. You're hiding behind rose bushes. I'm sweating each night, your face confronting me with its perennial presence.

Women weep under their black robes, they climb and throw flowers and rice instead of grenades, do listen, do you exchange arguments with me or with them, why is the sea green when we're talking, remembering my grandparents whom I never met - their dust was already spread over the highlands when I was born - and you keep asking if I'm still alive and I have no answer to that.

Currents meet in my body while it swims and I become water, part of water. The 'you' is always the 'I' so we inhabit each other in our irremediable singleness.

Deep in my sleep, water was running and there's war said

your voice, the future was being dismantled, and is love possible, your question hangs over my tranquility.

Yes, whose and whose beginning, comets are exploding on the side of wounded planets. Space is black-and-white movies, and your skin is catching fire.

Who is eating at the mountain when the moon sits on it? Before memory came into being there was an orange moon, there, and I went by it, walking, passenger of its sister-planet, and we were alone and why I don't know.

This heat is keeping the pressure on us, something will break loose in this speed, this terror.

THERE

When 'there' is 'here' and the air slows down you realize the sun's weight and as I know intimately the temperature we give up swimming and our eyes get heavy with humidity and you drag yourself to the door.

Could we talk across a border, on a barren field with the bronze age still around, the stone statues waiting for so long, now your shirt has mud and blood, and there's no water in sight.

Where were we, let's say in the last century? Under my fingers a slight stream is running to gardens and I wonder whose they are, and should we know by whom the orchards are owned? Can one possess the transient shimmering of the spring? Did the gods water their plants in this part of the world?

Do you, secretly, worship your father's framed picture or do I have to recall my mother's olive lamp, her icons over her bed, before the wars and the defeats which erased the sacred images, the sunlight which dried out - on the family papers - all the ink.

Do we each go through the same gestures in our kitchens; when tomatoes bleed do you feel triumphant?!

I know of days when people disappear, suddenly, like crates of fruit, and those who stay behind never move away from their windows ...

There, over there, across a street larger than many countries, something is taking off and stuffing the sky as much as the in-between spaces of my mind; over there where trains don't run ...

Regardless of the mobility of my surroundings, I notice that we're prisoners of love and hatred, look, the grass is bending under the wind, the storm has destroyed the villages, oh what was I going to say, we are queuing ...

THERE

Dust. Powder, Women wearing the rose colored make-up of death.

Do you love women? I mean do you witness their eagerness to walk ahead of you, courting disaster?

Where are you? From a hot July night comes the recollection of Damascus' covered markets, looking for you am I searching for my father's particular smell of tobacco and shave? Your traces are my own mind's blood … where is where, and always …

There, in this anxiety, I see the pallor of discarded manuscripts, and there's this glass of water you didn't drink, it's going to help some tropical growth in your sister's lungs and I will feel sorry, it would be useless, then will follow the celebration of the moon's darkest hour.

The wind is indeed howling within the summer's heat, invisible to all, treason thrives in such a weather and we wonder if we'll ever be free.

On the sea's unsteady surface large roads lead to yet more

water, the whistling leads to madness, from where I stand I'm cloud born of nowhere, similar to the colored edge of nothingness.

Don't. Do not. Not follow interdictions. If you would drown in my desperation you could become my other self, don't ever be what is me, or, for that matter, what is not me, this young man is coming through the walls, this fortress, carrying fried chicken and the tribe's message, telling what?

Do questions ever cease? Do the dead - some, at least - still wonder if the battle will be won, in spite of our contemplation of disappeared cities?

The earliest sun is like the setting one, everywhere, in Alexandria, who can tell, yet there is this gentle light ...

THERE

Birds flutter in splendor. The sun is setting over History. We have a war.

And why this presence, does this crowd concern you or me, can I have anything which will not be shared and what would it be?

This uncertainty? There are many gardens full of refugees who fled what, why, for their lives, the next encounters with what, let me ask.

You're fond of games, right here, why should fields of water evaporate so fast, as I see it from this position ...

Bits of space alternate with trunks of banana trees, threads of light move over the wound, my eyelashes filter sounds with urgency, an armored car breaks in, invasions create worry for the clouds, here, over here.

There

There, in front of me, without her, my amputated soul waits in a street-corner café, close to her, to her apartment, to her cell and prison and yet her queendom, and there in the music, are you in Europe, which Europe, the one negated, shadow-Europe, the one close to me, to us, the one you know which produced shouting poets, stuttering exiles, heroic travellers!

There, also where it hurts, ever so slightly, when a woman looks at him dreaming away his sailboat, and she dreaming of bed sheets and windows. Are you this man - or this woman - are you me, a self exploded and scattered, always kept aside, out of it, out of your sight, your purpose crossing mine; you're maybe the hidden seed of the earth, and me, the moon, it could be that I am Egypt reborn, yes, it could be, like the suns which are waiting beyond and behind all the probing machines that we send.

Are you, am I, is anyone *is-ing,* is anyone *be-ing,* is matter real, as real as we are, but aren't we real because we are dying and that matter is infinite and therefore not real?

Do you believe in enmity, destroy hills because you can't kill me, am I covering the earth with cement because something had died within before I was even born?

Oh how it hurts to witness the passage of time in terms of dead bodies and loves lost, and this distance, between us, unpassable, each knowing who is going to die first, where am I and where are you!?

THERE

In the green escape of my palace, over a bridge, under a canopy of opalescent light, through there, between dark branches and their shivering leaves, I'm lost in the scent of yellow roses, arrested by the range's filtering light.

Are you counting the years of my absence, remembering a first encounter, a place, an hour? Were we already enemies or did that happen later, not here, no, but at some point in the past, inside a room with closed shutters, and where has all this gone?

You were a boy on a bicycle, riding across an alley of icons, and I don't know why you were talking to no one but me.

When the weather becomes the whole of one's identity, lightning becomes speech and thunder residence. You're sitting on your house's stone floor watching the season's flow.

Where, here, on this earth, with the trains missing and the siege, I shall find out who's bringing me death, in this tunnel longer than the night.

There

In this my place time is shut off, death could be a beginning, a revolution's starting point: in the stillness surrounded by the highest trees, then the mountains, and beyond, the left-overs of History …

Here, I carry my *hereness* with my luggage; your body is decaying statue, forget Italy, its poisonous hillsides, let's cross that bridge before the falling of autumn's leaves.

You can, if you desire, sweep your floor with my family's parchments, but beware, the wind is rising, the air becoming metal. I live in a luminosity which renews its vigor.

There stands a tree. You're pushing the desert onward. With my legs folded under me I'm sitting, where? on the edge; over here, a sea of dust.

Deeper the oblivion deeper the hauntedness. We built unmeasurable empires. The horses, though, wanted the fields to be bordered fearing the salt mines.

Is there a language for lovers which doesn't need the lovers? Should we exchange genealogies over a poet's sealed body?

Do we have a land? Are the balconies ours, did we dangle our legs over the balustrade, were you a child with curling hair and me, impatient to grow?

We do worship the waves, don't we? Strange birds are chased away, I presume by the tribe. While battles rage, when long memory lines wait to be revived, the slaughter of shepherds goes on and death becomes a moving shadow on a screen.

I become a voracious animal, searching for self-affirmation on corpses - metaphorical for you and me - but real to those who left behind such decomposed traces.

HERE

What is *here?:* a place or an idea, a circle focused in God's eye, a cosmic wave's frozen frame, transient, doomed?

Here, where the heat mollifies, when the body surrenders before solicitations could reach it, and there, where the temperature boils the mind and makes it explode into sudden action; here is the point of no return ...

THERE

Armies engulf themselves in this uncertainty, horses reappear, but why, can this land go on creating mythologies while it lives under your jurisdiction, whose law, which mother-tongue?

In the canyons stars, as usual, outnumber water-holes, and I wonder if your children should walk on thorns and thistles, why did you elect such misery or did you find some grandeur to it?

Listen. Hear the wind. It's not the wolves who are howling but your men dreading your rage. I tell you that the future is today's price, then I see you laughing like my father used to.

There's granite in front of us. The mountain range is raising itself over the horizon and we're celebrating your victories, not ours.

Absurdly absurd this absurdity. Shadows, old companions, speak their own immensity. Why should I desire to undo Nature's simplest law - how can I remove your shadow from your body, and what good would that do to the nations I care for?

Horses will run from here to the signpost that you planted in the forest, the one nearest to this infinite desert, and this distance, between here and there, will be destiny's limitation.

One remembers that folded maps push countries aside, and next to this space valleys run to the sea, the colored one, and I'm in fear of an ambush while you think that pebbles are explosives; explosions are being heard from the river's other bank. The waters are running scared.

Some tender foliage covers my wound and I hear your arteries beat for there are highways in your bloodstream and we can't divert Time's flow nor tell the carnage to stop.

Darkness lies in your eyes, no, don't take projected shadows for secret services, I know as well as you did, once, over there, away from your birth place, that intelligence is for making bread, my steps will cross yours as much as my dust will raise your bones' ashes, and there's no wind in this harbor that we gave away for the rainfall that never happened, o my single night's thunder!

There, the sea is metallic. Primal is she, in this configuration of matter that created you, and me, and this atmospheric threat is for when, for what … our hands are weaving no happiness.

The sea under stress is boiling. You're new to these shores. Are you condemned to watch me lie on this bed, on the beach, over there, while space ebbs and flows under such a blanket of light that memory can only turn to sweat and any gleam of glory sound ridiculous ...

Has the human species left the here and now for a race toward the black holes? Do we acknowledge infallible failure? It seems that the breeze is caught up by the heat, that mountains can't transgress their assigned elevations.

Is it urgent to bring to consciousness one's darkest thoughts, silently, secretly, in cool air, through the streets? There are numerous monuments to melancholy, there, for him, for her, at the start, for me.

THERE

Or here, in early morning, how early you ask and I say let's get on with the day, a conversation is always a political thing because it involves two entities and the possibility of death interrupting it is always real, always there, and it could happen here, any time, by the stairs, the fountains, the music, and let's drink to things unsaid!

This wall, a circle in bronze sunk into the Earth, the earth sinking into itself; when I was drowning it was in a lake: you possessed - there, on this horizon of mine, on my left side - the road which led to my house. The birds were many and taking in the spring. Are you fond of our hills' particular freshness when the sea becomes a rug, that's the hour when the Bedus look at her with glee. You're always sitting across the table, scaring off my strange apprehensions.

In the heat, the earth's warming, this absorption of the sun's heat by the earth, I try to reach you, by the sweltering sea, such whiteness around me and such a distance between your letters and my answers!

Are you a son of mine, I'm sure you're not, and never will you be, it's always too soon, or too late, when the doors are closed, o the gentle movements of bodies on the sea's edge ...

Somewhere, you could have been my father's anger, he who never said a word after he reached forty, and you know, down there, under a white stone, whatever's left of his bones is asking for retribution, and the sea's answer is a swell, so very gentle, while the air is waiting for her to signal: sometimes immobility gives way to action, which actions ought we to desire, which city shall you inhabit, which would be conducive to my heart's rest? Where are we going from this point?

There's a breakthrough for the spirits which inhabit the sea. Shall they manage to lie between us, is the bus running aimlessly, there, where the poor don't need it? Some people eat dust others eat french fries ... where are these things happening?

What are the links between this space and me? Where do questions on the infinity of time and space lead to? Civilizations built on revenge shall disappear. So would the others. Could we then go on thinking?

A location. A site. Breathing needs miles of territory. If you want to reach the lions. (The breeze is in Egypt and the heat in Syria). The mountains are gone. Next to us storms are waiting. It will rain stones and bullets. Somewhere. Away from us. Oh how white is the sea when I think of you! Elsewhere, eventually, the dead will occupy no space.

You know what the heat does? Where? Right here and all

around. It melts one's spirit. Creates surrender. And to whom should one surrender? Would be easy to say to none. It would be a forbidden logic to say: to all. To the enemy? Who's my enemy? It's always tragic to have one. I can see anthills closing in.

Sharpening one's mind with the knife of despair. A blank space. An arrow. There, in front of my eyes, the void. Big and cold. We must reverse the seasons for accommodating these corpses. We're producing not water but blood, thirst being a priority.

Under this blanket of whiteness, on the sacred roads of lost powers a conversation is always a confrontation. Words are particles of air disseminated by the wind. So much silence within one's arteries: we can't move for this eternal battle. We haven't given it a name.

There, as far as my eyes can recognize a dot from a fly I see my accumulated journeys. Have I visited your country? Which one? For how long? Do you claim any place as your own? When dinosaurs' bones became as heavy as our houses these creatures died. Didn't they?

O lightning, where are we going to be on the Day of Judgment? This mountain will not divide. Nor this plain. Could rivers be named after their disappearance? Questions arise in my blood since Sumer's destruction. For how long? Cities dead or alive weigh down the spine. Where is the fragrance of the myrtle tree, has it found a place?

THERE

We're not charting the world, in a conversation, under some shade, our aim is to share bread and a piece of fish, and that's a consolation, but tell me where are all the men we knew?

Crickets sing the afternoon's glory, then the weather gets bad, there's flooding, but in whose country, with whose permission? Amplifiers tune in a war cry, yes, the forest is thick, but let's resume our talk, this meal, our defiant encounters are going to last as will our narrowly defined heritage.

In this circular room it's time to take a break, we entered it, so we have to stay, we can take a break from all this but we can't go, the coming century will disclose love's failure.

THERE

One. One plus one. The many added to the many. Proliferation: of the algae at patience's edge.

Here. On this wooden floor. There, on a moving surface and where they meet - if they do - there are trees and stones, the moon is bathing with its light this bit of a land.

A stroll on my turf, that's what's engaging you. Do I mind? Nothing is sure when it comes to you, to me, to us. To them.

Keep coming, if you can. It would be better if it were at night, let's think of a better way, there isn't any, the borders are closed and I'm not sleeping at home.

If we were not tied to a place what of us? I will introduce the sea into the frame and that would be tentative. Not an answer. Not a question.

Is place an illusion? Don't we go back and forth in a world invisible though as real as the table on which I'm having breakfast? And what about the no-place which precedes our birth and the one, very likely as illusory, into which death will take us?

Are we borrowing the here and now and if we are, from whom?

Do rights have foundations given the myriads of elements which make up in this avalanche of probabilities, the past, the present, my future and yours, the constant displacement of causes and effects, in the primordial chaos of passion, the sacrificial nature of Love, in the sea's blind beauty and the sun's demise; there was a preterritorial innocence, and there will be a silence, and everybody's final word, which won't be a word, no, no, at the beginning and at the end there's no word, no space, not even nothingness, not even the lack of it all.

THERE

The time-machine stares at us, leaving far behind the sea's whiteness. We're carried by the voyage, away from the race's stubbornness. Imagination will create a monument, one, at least, to the hour of forgiveness. Rivers do meet, waters submit themselves to the ocean's attraction, if it's true that the sun repeats its rise and its disappearance.

THERE

So close. Fire and flame. Could I know the wind's birth, the sun's falling out from its orbit, and the mountains surging over, never far from my vision?

Where? How is cunning operating over these hills? Why is the cat screaming and all these foxes running over terror's last frontier?

There, never on this planet, my right side's angel is trying to move in front of me and we're fighting this incessant battle and your tears are washing my feet. You're wounded, aren't you, you're falling on this autumn's dying leaves, let's keep the guns away, regardless of whose they are, we're praying to the same rain spirit under this untractable sky.

Listen. There's fatigue in your limbs, we walked for so long. Look, there's sand, look at it before your eyes fall asleep. Trust my hands, they'll give you a blanket, but where would you lie, didn't the Army teach you how to rest against a wall, I will not give you a bed of roses, nor a coffin, never, so take some shade under the oak tree.

What is love? We live it intimately but ignore what it is. It resembles space and time, and like these two concepts, it is clear, functional, and practically non-existent, and do I love you because of this proximity, this obsessive involvement? You filled my space for so long, snaked yourself in my waters, and I'm left with signs, and traces of you, exclusively, look, the sea is leaving, she's already beyond the horizon.

THERE

Again. Listen, while your ear is tuned to the sea, she who is mirroring her youth on her own waters ... Why is the Black ghetto so dark, in San Francisco, at dusk, while the ocean churns in its white fury and Africa wears a purple belt on her horizon?

Did Africa ship her lions to the Pacific, are we waiting for the impossible happiness to happen, and if it does, on which coastline, will the month be in spring or winter, will we rent a room with a view on the ocean, and catch a fever?

I closed my eyes, this morning, in front of your picture, your image having blurred my vision, and some ghost was standing there, a few feet away from my armchair, and the Shaker piece of furniture was saying oh yes, we heard about the past and its disappearance.

Are you still young or have you grown old, nearing your end, am I insensitive to your worries, but then could I dig into your mind like archeologists do, can I figure out its limits, are those recognizable to an alien spirit, are we going to dance, and what if you were beautiful, would we meet anonymously, with mistaken identities, considering that the sea is the realm of my peace and the residue of all questions?

Have you tried to rise high on air by your own means, angels do, it depends on their names, the heat helps, and there's an invocation, they outnumber us, over here, with a suffocating presence, we never talked about it, have we, and why, and who knows ...

THERE

Not too far from my house I used to play with the waves - where are they now? I was a child, then, the place is far away. They speak to me of other worlds, I care for this one, consisting of the chair I'm sitting on and the pain that tightens my heart, and the light falling right now outside the window. Where are your scissors, the ones, sharp and blue, used on your mother's dress?

Are you somewhere you can hear me, or are you dead, unreachable already, and does malediction follow, why do I assume that the season has changed, the heat subsided, would it be better for the dead if it rained on earth?

I hated you for so long in the inner territory that we inhabited together that you're now the negative print of my identity (no, not a shadow), the unwanted companion who becomes, o tragedy!, love's very substance.

There

Ongoing is the hour. The process of fragmentation is eating at its own instrument. The heat belongs to Egypt and the breeze to Syria. Let it be!

There, on the desert's intimate floor who's going to approach my inviolable space if not my enemy?

Thus, many nations at the end of their march will dwell in swamps, outside coherent discourse. The moment has arrived when they won't need specific boundaries. The desert brings together what cities divide.

There's pressure. The absoluteness of matter. *Parousia*. This beginning, the voyage ahead. The light's horizontality. The sun's truth (which truth?). Eternal hereness.

In an apocalyptic universe speech is doomed. Look at me while your eyes can see; they too will be no more.

Wherefrom the wind which brought treachery to the people? Questions are getting old but terrible the days when there won't be any.

The season's melancholy is ending on my heart - which I view as a mountain - and what's next, light and air at the temple's threshold. The divinities have departed, leaving the land - and the sound waves - in complete disarray, with a blinding sunrise overflowing into all of the mind's corners.

I am as close to my veins and arteries as they would allow, you're gone, the mountain is covered with clouds, maybe it ceased to exist, I lost my way, then it isn't fog, no, it's unnameable, and this sky, which isn't, is the mirror of my aberration.

THERE

There, in the wastes of the soul, within its repetitions, where we wonder if there are differences between the mind's inner chambers and the imagination's outer realms, lies the confrontation between the self and itself.

Where territory is pure memory, rarefied air, where a line is thinner than the horizon. I encounter the demands of definition, the pressure of realities which I thought weren't my own anymore.

Listen, we have to call you, bring back your attention to this particular place; we can abolish time, yet it doesn't seem capable to surmount spatiality, we cannot betray matter, win where the gods tried and failed.

There are stones in Greece, there's white marble in one's sleep there, where things move, where one can experience stirrings of freedom, you, a night visitor with infrared gear can see me while I can't see you, so the fight has no honor, what has to be killed is already dead, let's not waste the time left for those angels who want to mingle with humans; we scared them off, the land being poor and the imagination lacking, the gods won't punish us, we're of little importance.

We cannot confuse the signs, no, we can't, they will outlast us. Their nature requires that they remain clear, like the sky today, unbearably clear, creation occurs every morning, the signs are distributed over the horizons.

Moral impotence makes us successful. War is raw. Clearly so. It intensifies desire, the ultimate one, the one meant to annihilate what is and make happen what was not to be, turn the metaphysical enterprise of love into hate.

War is our dialogue. It brings explosions at home, debris of human limbs, booby-trapped love letters. We're sorrow's old veterans, having written lamentations on too many bones. Always the writing, that recorded silent voice which jumps generations to claim eternity for blood.

So what brings you back from over mountains, in July's aridity, under the sun's dominance, missing parents, divinities that we share, where is blind energy coming from, the earth, the sky, the void?

THERE

Under the impossible fortress, impossibility - standing - is holding the clouds under its spell, and in this impossibility, at a distance defined, who's looking at us? neither a god nor a piece of matter, but your desire for a deep sleep and my yearning for the end of this spilling of blood.

Over our heads sunrises defy the cannon's call, and later, beyond the castle, there's the northern land north of Northern Italy, and a river flowing East, over there there's Bosnia, where you had a home, and I had relatives, or was it the other way around, do I have to have a nationality in order to be human, and do you need to carry much paper on you if you wanted to dream, with open eyes, of mountains visited by birds ... do we need to own a name when the hungry call themselves Lack-of-Bread or St. John-the-dying?

There, in front of me, the music rises, Nono, Luigi Nono, who believed in the oneness of all, *Caminantes ... Ayacucho,* his nomadic sounds proliferating thunder on Africa's night, where's the hope that he placed in the simplicity of meanings while he staged the trumpets of an ongoing Apocalypse within the simultaneity of collective being?

It's already yesterday, I mean a second ago is as far back as an eternity of time, but over here, in the brotherhood of the telling, there's this hunger, those who need bread need roses too, and if I came to hear the music, I found the heart, little luminosities walked among us, from these valleys of tears is rising a smile under the first season's first rain, oh yes!, the over there and the over here belong to some continuum which glows at night from that fortress, all windows lit, all walls disappeared.

THERE

The horizon is flat and circular, above eye level. When the sea is silent the war is best heard. There are revolutions between us and the earth's turning. How lonesome the planets!

Between you and me there's plenty of air, of suspended desires, and memories in heroic quantities, in this tomb of a room and in the fabulous waterways of the arteries.

You loved Schubert and not Schumann, why? Does everything proceed from a delusion?

This time, within me, lies a body which died to the world and came to inhabit me. Absence pays a transient homage to the passing of time.

There

In this late hour, this island, this garden, what do we need?
When drops of water fall from your hands - after you washed
your face - your towel gets to be cool and calls for the
summer heat to cover me with the itinerant cloud's haze.

I wanted to be the room itself so you could know where to
find me; you wanted to be a horse, but nothing was built for
Arabia's poets.

People have become metallic. I can hear them demand
attention, but God surrendered to His own God. Nobody is
denying the ascensions and the voyage back. The desert is
blooming with the dew, the lesser divinities are giving a party.
We're left with voices.

There

We're always living in some season, aren't we? Seasons succeed each other. Today I saw some of the last remaining leaves fall from the linden trees and I thought of my own tears. There's no use in hurrying to point to the coming spring. The road ahead is quite long and empty. The sea is constant narrative. It's always a shadow, a double, which presents itself at restaurants' doors and such other grave-yards. Would the garden tell the new owners who I was and why I am no more?

Could I reach you - in whatever state of being you might be - did some entity of yours survive, even if with attributes alien to us, in places non territorial?

Heed my word, if you can, do deny your fate. I'm not asking for fullness, completeness, the fullness of resurrection, sit once more on your bed's edge, let's bring back the smells, the velvet, the bench, your breathing's regularity, my heart's pounding, the sweetest faring of the moment.

Which moment would you say, where did it go, why was your face so haggard during the spasms which were achieving a lingering oneness? That knowledge is branded on my brain.

Were we animals too earth-bound to fly? How can your solid form become air, or the script be preordained.

Who broke the thread, your lover? Remember, you had one, and she slid, and fell, the season sliding along, it scared you, you were a casualty of war, I know ...

We did enter paradise, didn't we? We did reverse the banishment, haven't we. Such distances are short.

There

The mother of battles, yes, the battlefield, the war. Some sleep with their tie around their neck, the hangman's noose.

The city is an army on the march. Trees wear their majesty like a banner, they form an honor guard. On the enemy's bulletin boards we have nothing to report. We fancy ourselves to be solid objects thrown into collisions but the situation is different.

There's a highway that links us to the dark kingdom and we take it every so often. In a grayness evenly distributed, we go towards people who move carefully behind translucent veils. There, we the living engage the dead in conversations: their voices are hushed. There is greyness to these voices too, and a strange though quiet urgency. We pursue the silent communications that we used to have in times already ancient, and sometimes we lie between them, with no sleep, no waking. Theirs are powerful (and discrete) presences to whom we delegate our consciousness. Very few words are pronounced but the unavoidable dialogue goes on in all the worlds, those we know with familiarity and those whose existence we perceive by osmosis, as if we were bathing in some permanent penumbra.

THERE

Such as two trees planted next to each other, under an ageing moon, we're prisoners of a circularity. Remembrance needs primeval forgiveness. Energies, in their acceleration, will break the heavens.

There, where there's fire, when the fear of death coincides with spring, are we going to be doomed to be lovers who could never meet, restless as the sea's surface?

O devastated creation! Love of love, eyes filled with dust, the burned body's particles dispersed, end of end and end's ending brought about by the sun's decisions, o the resurrection of desire after the body's destruction! If you aren't, how can the soul not die?

THERE

Before its setting it was young and made us luminous; now, while we're lying against a pillow and the light is coming through the window, this transfigured sun, ruler of Egypt, ancient and ever-new daughter of the Nile, descends on water and sand and moves on to Earth's unstable horizon.

Where was it, at which hour, why was I waiting amidst such splendor, wishing the twin disappearance of the lover and the city? What's the use of crying over Alexander's beauty when he's buried in marble and gold? Is memory divine presence made out of flesh, a mind-creation which lasts a few years in which there are a few privileged hours, and where is that knowledge which solely matters - my body's with its shadow, and my soul's, if I had one?

What's in store, what's eternity doing? Why such cruelty when the weather is fine and the body intact?

We have experienced ecstasy in the dark (the one with the other), mostly in the night, in the here and now of cities of heat and sweat. We also did die many times, didn't we, of love and separation, so that when the end will come it will be a comfortable, though perverse, homecoming. We did reach the absolute, didn't we, for a handful of hours, somewhere in between, in between 'you' and 'I'.

THERE

Enmity made us lovers, and you died of it, there, on the line, between ocean and sand. In that night you met your darkest encounter. An overdose of happiness kills as surely as lightning.

There, a procession of fires proceeded towards the forest. It needed additional fuel to feed its passion. Is destruction an inseparable component of love?

On my American screen I saw the Vietnamese peasant who was running and on whose skin napalm on fire was closer than his wife: war, which liberates and kills those it liberated, joined us forever.

THERE

From the primeval waters we arose - you and I, from the beginning we went on a search and when the gardens grew we looked together for a shade, didn't we?

From the desire to live we arose and built nations, didn't we?

Then we were visited by a creature not named by any of the gods and we called it Death, and it took power over us, and autumn on its first day started to shed yellowish leaves on our beds; then the trees stared at their own bareness and we didn't come to their aid, did we?